Cold water cure

Cold water cure

Claire Orchard

Victoria University Press

TE WHARE WĀNANGA O TE ŪPOKO O TE IKA A MĀUI

VICTORIA
UNIVERSITY OF WELLINGTON

VICTORIA UNIVERSITY PRESS
Victoria University of Wellington
PO Box 600 Wellington
http://vup.victoria.ac.nz

National Library of New Zealand Cataloguing-in-Publication Data

Orchard, Claire.
Cold water cure / Claire Orchard.
ISBN 978-1-77656-057-8
I. Title.
NZ821.3—dc 23

Printed by Printlink, Wellington

for Greg

Contents

iii

Notes

'Hang on' is a found poem, a quote from Ali Williams during the All Blacks 2011 World Cup Campaign.

'You played 2 hours to die like this?' is a collection of quotes from video games.

'Deltic 1989's advice on train photting etiquette' is a found poem, sourced from a trainspotting forum: http://www.railforums.co.uk/showthread.php?t=42322

★

The italicised words and phrases in 'In the library with Darwin's red notebook' are from a notebook Darwin wrote in during his time on board HMS *Beagle*.

The left-aligned sections of 'Voyages' are from Darwin's *The Voyage of the Beagle* (1839/1905).

The events described in 'Condor', 'Ithacaia', 'Viewing such men' and 'The ferry slave' are based on descriptions recorded by Darwin in *The Voyage of the Beagle*.

'The Diary of Mrs Edmund Lumb' is based on the recollections of Anne Lumb Macdonell, as published in Reminiscences of Diplomatic Life (London: Adam & Charles Black, 1913), of a family story she was told about events that occurred during Darwin's visit to her parents' home in 1837.

'Upon this matter of the heart' draws inspiration and phrases from two notes Darwin wrote in the months leading up to his marriage proposal to Emma Wedgewood in 1838. These have been published as Appendix 4 of *The Correspondence of Charles Darwin*, vol. 2, 1837–1843 (Cambridge, UK: Cambridge University Press, 1987).

The lines in 'The unravelling' are from letters Darwin wrote while working on his manuscript for *On the Origin of Species*.

The details of 'Dr Gully's Cold Water Cure' are sourced from 'The hydrotherapy and infamy of Dr James Gully', an article by William E. Swinton published in *Canadian MA Journal*, vol. 123 (20 December 1980). Darwin underwent the 'water cure' at Malvern, Worcestershire, and at his home in Kent, setting up the equipment required in his backyard, from 1849 until the end of 1851.

The lines in 'My Dearest Emma' are all extracted, unaltered aside from line breaks and ordering, from Darwin's letters to his wife Emma during the final illness of their daughter Annie, who died the month after her tenth birthday. Annie's writing case and its contents were kept by the Darwin family in remembrance of Annie.

The untitled haiku and the untitled Fibonacci poem were extracted, with the assistance of a computer programme, from an electronic text version of *On the Origin of Species*.

'Battle of the vegetables' was the title of a picture drawn by one of Darwin's young children on the reverse side of a draft of *On the Origin of Species*. Only around thirty such pages survive; many did so only because Darwin gave them to his children to draw on and then kept the pictures.

The facts in 'The billiard table' are sourced from the second volume of Janet Browne's excellent biography *The Power of Place* (Princeton, NJ: Alfred A. Knopf, 2002) and from letters in the Darwin Correspondence Database: www.darwinproject.ac.uk.

Many of the phrases in 'Early morning on the Sand-walk' are extracted from *On the Origin of Species* (1859).

'A short note from brother Erasmus in London' is an extract from a letter from Erasmus Darwin to his brother Charles in December 1862. The full text of the letter can be found on the Darwin Correspondence Database.

'A cipher of a man' is a found poem; the text is from Algernon Charles Swinburne's short parody 'Dethroning Tennyson: A Contribution to the Tennyson–Darwin Controversy', published in *Nineteenth Century* 23 (January 1888): 127–30.

The various voices in 'Twelve voices over five courses' are based on extracts from Thomas F. Glick's *What about Darwin?* (Baltimore, MD: The John Hopkins University Press, 2010).

Darwin's experiments concerned with establishing whether or not earthworms have a sense of hearing are described in his book *The formation of vegetable mould through the action of worms, with observations on their habits,* published in 1881, the year before his death. Some of the phrases in 'Bee' can be traced back to comments Darwin made about bees, pike, and weaver birds in the same book.

★

The title of 'This way for the gas' is borrowed from Tadeusz Borowski's short story collection *This Way for the Gas, Ladies and Gentlemen* (1959; translated to English from the Polish 1967).

The line lengths in 'Fully informed' are based on data from a graph published in the *Dominion Post* in 2011.

i

Hang on

I think we're getting ahead of ourselves here.
Last time we got ahead of ourselves,
we shot ourselves in the foot
then we did it again a few years before that –
shot our other foot.
We're just trying to leave our feet on.

Sharpening

They all know, the little ones
because they've all tried it,
what happens to the pencils
when you push them,
blunted end first,
into the hole and turn them
against the blade,
and yet today I feel it
again, the amazement
offered by one small boy bringing me
the finger he has shorn, the nail shredded,
blood dark and oozing from the tiny wound.
Did you put your finger in the sharpener?
Did you catch it against the blade?
I ask these questions without thinking,
tearing open a band-aid.
He's six, the number of perfection.

Two points of contact

You must make sure you always have
two points of contact,
the father called after his daughter
who was dashing off ahead
down the stairs.
What? She screwed up her face.
A foot on the tread, one hand on the rail:
two points of contact,
he explained.
But that means (she said slowly,
as if speaking to one very young)
if I take my hand off the rail,
I can't move at all.
Exactly, he said.

We're all five

At the start we're all lost. Unloaded, we walk in that way.
But pretty soon we've worked out where our allocated spaces are,
can find a place to stand not touching anyone else.
Did you notice the signs? There are moments that fly apart like firework
explosions, everything colliding with its opposition, sparking
fights for territory or position. One person's inflammatory
gambit is accepted by another who's been
hoarding aggravation and it's all on, until someone else
intervenes with a collection of pencils in a painted tin. Redirected, we all
jump up in unison, getting to it now even as one of us
kneels hard on another one's foot, quite by accident and
look no one's perfect. One day we begin to notice
more details, like how the spaces between words show something
not clear to us yet, that has to do with meaning
or understanding. Powerful, we push them apart with our fingers,
pioneering the ideal gap. Too spread out at the start, they close up
quite quickly really and we're away, writing ourselves
right down the page and over the back until
someone mentions lunch.
Time was we didn't know the names for things but now we're
utterly absorbed by placing cubes in rows and counting them, with
variegating paintings of our favourite things, at least until we're thinking
we'd like to go home soon. Just then someone reveals their
X-ray vision, which proves a distraction from this sudden
yearning. Waving our hands wide we confide that well we have a
zillion super powers you know. Maybe more.

Egg

What people often don't realise, my grandfather said abruptly,
while we were sitting on a bench at the playground,
is that parenting involves taking
a lot of split-second decisions.

I remember one time we were down here,
just me, your mother and your uncle. Maybe
they were five and seven,
it could have been six and eight,

but there they were on that whirligig thing
going round and round for ages and suddenly
I picked up a pebble, weighed it in my hand,
and realised I could do it,

I could get it between the two of them
while they were spinning around, as long as I timed it
just right. And so I tried it. Managed to miss
your mother all right. Hit your uncle in the side of the head.

Perhaps it wasn't the best idea. Certainly your grandmother
thought not, when I got them home and she saw the egg.
But you make your call, don't you? And just think,
if I'd pulled it off, what a story they'd've had to tell.

Truth to power

Upon arrival I survey the field:
one five-year-old has retreated
to the anonymity of the cubicle,

the other, round-faced, mouth a perfect o,
is looking up at me from his position
beside the sink.

Were you fighting? No, we weren't.
He shakes his head emphatically.
We weren't fighting. We were just deciding

who's the boss. His eyes are round too,
bright and glossy with
the righteous light of truth.

You played 2 hours to die like this?

It's a-me, Mario! Thank you, Mario, but our Princess
is in another castle. This is your fault.
And all the cake is gone. You don't even care, do you?
My scythe. I like to keep it next to where my heart used to be.
The right man in the wrong place can make
all the difference in the world. Oh, hi. So,
how are you holding up? BECAUSE I'M A POTATO!
I used to be an adventurer like you,
then I took an arrow in the knee. What is a man?
A miserable little pile of secrets. Everything
is permitted. Everything is teetering on the edge
of everything. Snake? Snake? I feel asleep.
War has changed. War never changes. Would you kindly . . .
I have metal joints. Beat me up and win 15 Silver Points.
We may be pirates, but we're not barbarians.
We'll let them keep the toilet paper. Wait,
that's not how it happened. I am error.
Wakka wakka wakka. Wyonk wyonk wyonk.
Why not take a break? You can pause the game by pressing +
It's dangerous to go alone; take this! It's super effective!
You are likely to be eaten by a grue. Hold on a second.
Assassin is a chick? How did I miss that? Why,
that's the second biggest monkey head I've ever seen!
Conglaturation! Oh look, another visitor. Stay a while . . .
Stay FOREVER! You have died of dysentery. Nothing
is true. You have completed a great game! A winner is you.

Shorty

The day we met in the classroom you were just five and I was some thirty
years older.

Years have passed. I will admit, you have become much
less short

and yes now, I concede, there is
some debate

as to which of us should
keep the nickname.

One day, no doubt,
I will accept it with good grace

and you
will go tall into the world and do great things.

Shortly but please not just yet,
my dear young friend.

History

I hear him on the radio,
the man who used to be a boy
in my sixth-form class
at our well-below-average high school.
Now he heads up a multi-million-dollar
finance company. As his well-modulated
vowels explain the interesting
situation the organisation now finds
itself in, I know it's him,

I recognise the name
and it's History again, Friday afternoon,
that final double period,
that last game of *Risk*,
the four of us leaning forward on those old-style
school chairs, game pieces and board laid out
across some sort of box and that boy opposite,
smiling so sweetly,
getting ready to stab me in the back
from his position in the Ukraine.

Settling for Action Man

That summer, blond Cindy (mine),
and blonder Barbie (borrowed,
belonging to my absent older sister)
spent many a weekend afternoon
on Niamh Guinness's back lawn, partying hard
with Niamh's brunette Cindy.
Yes, we keenly felt the lack
of a Ken doll. A Ken would have
brought us closer to a gender balance,
but Kens were in short supply
in our neighbourhood.
A Ken, with his blond hair and permasmile,
would have provided the perfect foil
for any, indeed all, of the female dolls,
despite his squishy head.
Without a Ken, we had to make do
with an Action Man borrowed
from Niamh's oblivious older brother.
Action Man, although ruggedly handsome,
had visible hinges on his elbows and knees,
and his unwavering expression
of utter disdain made it harder for us
to pretend he fancied any of the girls.
Still, we had him plant long, hot, plastic kisses
upon their small, pink-painted mouths,
all the while pressing his camo-clad body
suggestively against them. Of course
the anatomical deviations of the participants
their obvious shortcomings and exaggerations
meant from the outset any action we choreographed
fell well short of our cherished romantic notions.
We made do. It proved valuable preparation.

Don't let me be misunderstood

There's a young man at the next table wearing
my T-shirt. I mean he's wearing a T-shirt
the same as one of mine. I have a T-shirt just like his.
Only smaller. And his fits differently,
on account of his flat-chestedness.

He could be my son. I mean he's not, but he could be,
he's young enough is what I mean. He looks a bit
disconcerted, I think he's noticed me looking at him.
Probably thinks I'm a cougar. Not an actual cougar.
I'd hate to be misconstrued. After all,
he could almost be my son. I'll look away now,

check out the flowers hanging from the ceiling.
They're plastic, so not actual flowers.
The colours are quite garish but I guess
they occur in nature. The colours I mean,
not the flowers. Flowers like that don't exist.

He's doing the crossword. I mean he's filling it in.
With a pen. He's not very good. At the crossword,
I mean. His head's bobbing up and down
as he counts the spaces. He's frowning, it doesn't fit.
I'd offer him a hand, but he might misunderstand,
plus he's doing the cryptic. I'm no good at those.

She walks

ahead of me to a rhythm set
    by the buds in her ears and I follow
the swing of her hips in short shorts
    hoping to guess

the tune from her sway.
    Her black cheesecloth shirt matches
her black Chuck Taylor shoes and I think
    how beautiful,

in this slight rain, the shirt will turn
    translucent soon, her legs will sheen
and her hair, already wet, will drip
    dark snakes down her back.

Legendary creature

for Alice

Your many-winged laundry rack
resembles a pale, anorexic albatross
doubled over
in the open boot of the car, resting

on the dark green sea of your nylon suitcase,
cresting waves of
tied-up plastic shopping bags packed tight
with folded sheets and pillowslips,
extra blankets because
those hostel rooms get cold.

You say come on, it's time to go and
I snap a quick photo, a beauty: you
on the driveway, pulling out
your circus strongman poses.

Poetry masterclass

Embassy Theatre, 2013

The woman who arrived late and sat beside me
did not have a copy of the poems but accepted an offer
to share mine. And so it began.

She referred to the presiding poet as Bill and,
before he'd begun to address himself to the first poem,
had taken a pen and scored briskly through three of its lines.

Audience feedback abounded. One woman down the front
wanted a simile rehabilitated as a metaphor, another
recommended the removal of the word 'cocked',

someone waving urgently from the back row requested
the addition of a comma. The woman beside me scribbled
'no commas is GOOD' on our copy of the poem.

So it went, until the final line of the final poem drew forth
a final criticism for what appeared to be an unwarranted
change in tense. *It's subjunctive* the woman beside me muttered.

As the poets shuffled from the stage I waited
in my seat, fannying about fake-texting friends,
hoping she would give back the poems.

Leaving the theatre, I sidestepped a trike driven by a runaway toddler.
The mother's face apologised for her girl, who, pedalling hard,
was targeting the harbour at the end of the road.

Deltic 1989's advice on train photting etiquette

As a rule, when I intend to hang around photting at a station
for more than an hour or so, I tend to seek out the duty station manager
and ask their permission.

I find that if you politely ask then you normally get
cooperation, also the staff then know you are there
and what you are doing.

I especially make an effort to do this if I'm at a mainline station
(my usual haunt being Newark Northgate) because then I can't be mistaken
for a terrorist doing reconnaissance or something like that.

The manager is generally OK with it, but they usually stipulate
that staff cannot appear in any photographs, which to me is fair enough;
I'm there to phott trains, not staff.

Also, as mentioned, tripods aren't advised as they can get in the way;
I never have and never will use a tripod
as I prefer 'free hand' photography.

Most places I've been have generally been very good,
with the exception of a misunderstanding at Crewe after a shift change
(but that is another very very long story).

Crisis management

It's a good day for keeping the doors closed,
for staying away from windows, for free-streaming
black-and-white movies, Westerns, preferably,
because today's about crisis management,
and in your classic Western there's always some guy
in a black hat fixing to take over your once peaceful town,
or buy up your struggling ranch for a pittance
so his cigar-smoking boss can exploit it for oil.
You have a train of canvas-covered wagons
full of starving orphaned children to get through
a narrow, loose-earthed canyon before nightfall,
before that posse of tobacco-spitting,
dark-eyebrowed outlaws catches up with you.

Pencil drop

Pencils, sour, damp
like hymns, yet cleaner,
a breaking sight.
Hula hoops in red and black
negotiating night.
Look, preserve the news
through furniture.
A plank will do it.

In the library with Darwin's red notebook

Six floors up the windows show signs of smeary contact,
salty particles like prickly kisses blown up from the harbour
from a seafarer's bearded lips while, open on the table,
ocean-stained pages of your notebook drift,

pencilled lines, smudgy in places, your handwriting untidy,
at times unclear. I make out *inosculation* with a single line
through it, representation added above, but what word is that,
starting with *s*? You underlined *gradual* with a firm stroke,

scored another word until it was unreadable. So we go
on, you retreating as I advance over pebbles, beached somewhere
you do not name, in the air a tang of distance and discovery
spiked with your unwillingness to doubt your own eyes.

Upon closing the book I see, scrawled across the back cover
in brown ink, in your hand: *nothing for any purpose*. As if,
despite your growing understanding, your final impulse
was to camouflage these shipboard findings.

Voyages

1

Close to the brink, where the current
seemed to be deflected upwards
from the face of the cliff,
I stretched out my arm, and immediately
felt the full force of the wind:
an invisible barrier, two yards in width,
separated perfectly calm air from a strong blast.

> I scrambled up the steep path
> to the summit of Makara Hill and stopped,
> breathless. Out to sea, two fishing dinghies formed
> punctuation marks on the wide blue page.
> The day was so bright, the air so clear
> I could make you out, I fancied,
> on the distant, inky hills of the other island:
> close to the brink, a man-shaped smudge
> with one arm outstretched.

2

A man on horseback
having thrown his lazo
round the horns of a beast
can drag it anywhere he chooses,
the animal ploughing up the ground
with outstretched legs.

I drove our Toyota into a blackbird; it shot out
from between two parked cars
thumped into our front grill.
I looked in the rear-view mirror, hoping
to see it reflected in flight
from the scene. Just stunned,
I lied to my son.

When we got home it was there all right, bloody
feathers awry, yellow intestines wound
like kitchen twine around the bumper,
the soles of its feet pointing skyward.

3

No one here possesses
a watch or a clock.
An old man is employed
to strike the church bell by guess.

Here, wrist watches
are becoming archaic.
People seem increasingly
to be troubling me
for the time.

4

It seems almost a pity
to kill such nice little animals
for, as the Gaucho said
while sharpening his knife
on the back of one,
armadillos are so quiet.

I spotted a tiny, white-tailed spider
amongst my salad leaves,
a fast mover. Eventually
I managed to corral it onto
the thin edge of my knife.

5

Both parties were laughing,
gaping at each other,
we pitying them
for giving us good fish for rags,
them at finding people so foolish
as to exchange such splendid ornaments
for a good supper.

In exchange for €29 plus international postage
I will receive a rectangular prism of wood
the size of a small packet of tea bags,
painted matt black and christened
nothing. It is designed to sit on my mantelpiece
as a dumb reminder
that I want for *nothing*.

6

She remarked how strange
to dine with an Englishman
for as a girl, at the mere cry
'Los Ingleses', every soul,
carrying what valuables they could,
had taken to the mountains.

                    I once loved an Englishman
                      who failed utterly to see
                    what all the fuss was about
                         right up until the day
                      he found himself alone
                          with the silverware.

7

'El Turco', tail feathers erect,
pops from one bush to another
on stilt–like legs with uncommon
quickness, as if aware
of its most ridiculous figure
and ashamed of itself.

Somewhere in this picture,
if you can find it,
is the figure of a man,
so the caption said. I looked,
but couldn't find a figure of a man,
only a large rock
and a few scrubby bushes.

8

In five minutes
more than fifty mosquitoes
alighted on my hand
forming a black, sucking, mass.

Every weekday afternoon
the owner of Pirie Street Dairy
leaves his past–dated pies
out on the pavement.
The pigeons peck at such manna
while people mutter and shoo,
picking a path through.

9

I had thought for a moment
I was eating a local delicacy,
namely a half-formed calf,
long before its proper time of birth,
but happily it turned out to be Puma,
which is remarkably like veal in taste.

I was starting on my scrambled eggs
when two international students
sat down at the next table.
One took photos on her phone
of the colourful plastic fruit lights
strung across the ceiling, while the other
pointed at my plate of yellow on toast
and asked the waitress to explain.

10

On one of these columns of ice
a frozen horse was sticking
as if on a pedestal, but with its hind legs
straight up in the air, as if it had fallen
head first into a hole during snow.

I stop by the grave of the man
who fell head first into a hole during snow
to check the letters of his name
are still sharp and toothpaste white,
that the caretaker has electric-trimmered the grass
away from the edges of the stone.

11

Papilio feronia
is the only butterfly
I have ever seen
that uses its legs
for running.

The last time I saw him was on the cliff edge
of a deadline. I ran through the town, ridiculous,
holding a small casket of green Californian grapes
aloft. Bedridden, he said he was done
sacrificing fruit upon the ruined altar of his throat.

He was not in the room he had hoped
would be his dying room, the one with
a bay window overlooking the street. Instead
he was closer to the bathroom,
with a view of corrugated-iron fence.

12

There is much bloodshed,
the habit of constantly
wearing a knife
being the chief cause.

At dinnertime there's
blurred, jerky footage of men wearing
masks and machine guns,
of bodies being dragged off the backs of utes.

13

A fox, said to be peculiar to the island
and very rare, failed to notice me
walking up quietly behind him.
I was able to knock him on the head
with my geological hammer.

I cannot conclude that the dead
pass on or over anything.
No, not to the other side.
Only a moment, or years ago,
they were alive and now are dead.

14

Captain Fitz Roy could never ascertain
that the Fuegians have any distinct belief
in a future life. They sometimes bury their dead
in caves, sometimes in the mountain forests.
We do not know what ceremonies they perform.

I make a ceremony, now and then,
of reading Tennyson's *In Memoriam*;
his tortured, imperative
'thou wilt not leave us in the dust'
makes me ache, not for myself
but for his sake.

15

In this quiet spot
sailors from a sealing vessel
murdered their captain;
we saw his skull
lurking among the bushes.

Since the storm,
council workers, bless them,
have been busy clearing
fallen trees, flushing out
the dark corners.

16

In order to secure tortoises
it is not sufficient to turn them
like turtle, for they are often
able to get on their legs again.

My fifth-form science teacher
dismissed death as
the thing even the most imbecilic among you
(we all looked at each other)
will succeed at. Life now,
she said, warming her bum on the radiator,
success at THAT will elude most of you,
I'm afraid. She smiled at us then.

17

A moonlit night on deck,
clear heavens, the dark
glittering sea a dead calm,
the heaving surface polished
like a mirror and all still save
the occasional flapping of the canvas.

> *Over us all hangs the same sky*
> the science teacher announced
> out of the blue-grey Friday afternoon;
> we were studying clouds at the time.
> Afterwards I stood at the school gate,
> rolling my ankles this way, then that,
> one, then the other, not really thinking
> about any of it, waiting on the rain.

18

Everywhere my compass created
unbounded astonishment;
that I, a perfect stranger,
should know the road to places
where I had never been.

Running around the bay in the windy dark
I met a man in a pinstriped suit
walking backwards,
but in the same direction.
He frowned at me,
shook his head, shouted
where are you even going?

Condor

A cleric's collar of feathers at his neck,
black wings fully extended,

surely they span eight feet from tip to tip,
held in perfect stillness,

thermal currents powering his sweep,
he descends, glides down, until

he's so close I imagine I feel his pulse
throbbing in the displacement of the air.

Holding on to my hat, I tip my head back
and see how his head, neck and tail move much more

than I expected, how his wings seem to act
as a fulcrum. For nearly half an hour

I watch him hunt over mountain and river,
the outlines of his terminal feathers dark

against the sky, until, with a single flap,
he ascends too high for my eyes to follow.

Near Lima

There you are, face up on an open plain,
following the reeling flight of carrion-hawks
sweeping in circles, the outlines of their wide wings
distinct against the blue sky.

Somewhere I read that, day to day, most of us
rarely raise our eyes more than fifteen degrees
above the horizon. Here tonight, nowhere near Lima,
each weary pedestrian

focuses on straight-ahead except
at street corners, where we turn our heads.
The yellow-lit windows
of the buildings tightly hem

and I admit I only look up now because
I'm thinking of you. I find it dizzying when I do,
the yawning weight of that cathedral dome
of bruised purple sky, wheeling on.

Ithacaia

April 8, 1832

Everything is motionless
save for the butterflies
and it is powerfully hot.

Beneath a rising moon
our guide tells the story
of a runaway slave,

an old woman who threw
herself from this summit
rather than submit.

In a Roman matron
this would be
the noble love of freedom;

in the negress it is
mere brutal obstinacy.
We continue on our way,

the distant and sullen roar
of the sea scarcely breaking
the stillness of this night.

Viewing such men

near Wollaston Island
we pulled alongside
six Fuegians in a canoe.
Poor wretches,
their growth stunted,
hideous faces bedaubed
with white paint,
skins filthy, greasy,
hair entangled,
voices discordant,
gestures violent;
one can hardly
make oneself believe
they are fellow creatures.

The ferry slave

I talked loudly, making signs
with my hands, endeavouring
to make him understand.

When my hand passed near his face
he, thinking me about to strike,
dropped his own hands to allow it.

From the diary of Mrs Edward Lumb of Buenos Ayres

Dear Mr Darwin is presently our guest,
although in fact he is away
for at least a fortnight, journeying to Quilmes,
near to Uncle John Yates' place,
on the trail of a mammoth shell.

It does seem incongruous:
a voyage of significant scientific discovery
(as Edward assures me it will prove)
employing for transportation a ship named after a dog.
My mother's aunt had a beagle: a clumsy creature
inclined to carrying a vast excess of weight,
and ultimately contributing nothing of use to the world.

I'm afraid, in Mr Darwin's absence,
I have committed an unintended crime,
one I hope he will forgive.
But the strange stench emanating
from the guest room became unbearable –
the housemaid had taken to avoiding the room entirely –

until finally, yesterday, I tackled the matter,
uncovered the culprit, lying supine in a drawer:
the decaying body of a small, dead mole
native to this area, although almost extinct,
wrapped carefully in a white cambric handkerchief.
Straight away I hurled it into the bedroom fire,
and it was only as I stood, shuddering still,
watching the funerary flames take hold
that I realised what I had done.
Oh, I cannot tell him myself.
Edward must be the one to do it.

Upon this matter of the heart

my poor vacillating brain is almost entirely decided. Although
it will mean less money for books. To travel further still appeals,
yet children are a comfort they say, a wife a better companion
than a dog. That I will be unable to read in the evenings

perhaps does not matter, as the expense of books is too high
anyway. Ah, but the cost of furnishing a house. The loss of freedom
to do as one pleases, to learn French, to go up in a Balloon.
Geological work will fall to morning calls. There are health benefits;

the married man lives longer. I will not indolently take
a country house and do nothing. I will need to find a job,
one that yet allows time for observations, for experiments.
Best not London. I would lose access to the countryside and

be required to visit relatives. Mexico, maybe, first? Though money.
No. It must be travel *or* marriage. Never mind, only think:
a nice soft wife on the sofa. Perhaps a Professorship?
The outskirts of Cambridge can be pleasant. A fish out of water

but we will avoid poverty, and that will be my first duty to our
children. What if we have many children? The expense,
the responsibility. The quarrelling. And yet, what alternative?
Solitude? A flat near Regent's Park? A groggy old age, friendless.

No, there is many a happy slave. I shall make the best, abandon
single life for one tethered, lovingly, to another.
Unless. Is it too violent a change to undertake?
But, if one does not wed, one misses out on the excellences

of a good woman, a clean house, a hearth of one's own. No,
I am convinced. Somehow, through all, I will keep on.
My intent is to focus upon Zoology.
A wife will be a vast help in organising notes.

The unravelling

In a gin palace in the borough
I have done a black deed,
among a set of pigeon fanciers:
murdered an angelic little fantail.

I have done a black deed:
lumps of cyanide of potassium
murdered an angelic little fantail,
for I mean to make skeletons.

Lumps of cyanide of potassium
half an hour before putting in the pigeon,
for I mean to make skeletons
to trace the gradual changes.

Half an hour before putting in the pigeon,
I cannot see this as false,
to trace the gradual changes
in the formation of a pigeon.

I cannot see this as false:
it seems preposterous that a maker of a universe,
in the formation of a pigeon,
should care about the crop of such a bird.

It seems preposterous that a maker of a universe
would aim to please man's fancies,
should care about the crop of such a bird.
Whatever holds good, I cannot see that this is false.

I have use of a very large, damp bottle
among a set of pigeon fanciers,
for I mean to pick apart the bones of birds
in a gin palace in the borough.

Dr Gully's Cold Water Cure

Five am,

patient to strip naked
and cold-water-soaked sheets
to be wound around the body

these in turn
to be covered over
with blankets.

Wait one hour,
strip once again.

Make an application of iced spring water,
one swift dousing,
from a bucket positioned
directly above the head.

Encase belly and lower back
in a wet girdle;
dress otherwise in warm clothing.

Undertake briskly
the five-mile walk from well to well,
taking draughts of water from each.

Sit for extended periods
before a hot lamp
to induce profuse sweating.

Breakfast should be dry biscuits,
water;
dinner always
boiled mutton and fish,
water.

No alcohol. No snuff. No work.

My Dearest Emma

My own dear how it did make me cry
to read of your going to Annie's garden for a flower.

Our poor child has been fearfully ill;
as ill as a human being could be,

you would not in the least recognise her,
her poor hard, sharp pinched features.

I could only bear to look at her by forgetting
our former dear Annie;
here is nothing in common between the two.

She has not had wine, but several spoon-fulls of broth,
& ordinary physic of camphor & ammonia –
Dr Gully is most confident there is strong hope.

*

I am assured Annie is several degrees better.
This morning she is a shade too hot,
but the Dr thinks her going on very well.

*

You must not suppose her out of great danger.
She keeps the same; just this minute she opened her mouth
quite distinctly for gruel – & said that is enough.

She has slept most tranquilly almost all afternoon,
perhaps too tranquilly.
We have bathed her again with vinegar.

★

An hour ago I was foolish with delight,
pictured her to myself making custards
(whirling round) as, I think, she called them.

I told her I thought she would be better
& she so meekly said thank you.

★

Poor Annie is in a fearful mess,
but we keep her sweet with Chloride of Lime;

she asked for orange this morning,
the first time she has asked for anything except water.

★

3 o'clock. She is going on very nicely
& sleeping capitally
with breathing quite slow.

★

We have changed the lower sheet,
cut off the tail of her chemy.
She looks quite nice.

Got her bed flat & a little pillow
between her two bony knees.
She is certainly now going on very well.

*

A low and dreadful fever.
Poor dear little Annie.
It is all over.

We must be
more and more to each other,
my dear wife.

How essential it
is in a flock of white sheep
to destroy a lamb.

A greater number
perish in the egg than are
able to get out.

It is difficult
to comprehend the meaning
of such facts as these.

No one ought to feel
surprise at much remaining
as yet unexplained.

Smooth

Tonight, my jaw aches;
I think it's something to do
with too much scrolling through
On the Origin of Species, underlining
all the evolutionary haiku
hiding there, and

it may also be related to the way
the doctor who had my skull x-rayed
when I was nine
told my mother over my head
that my jaw was *grossly deformed*.
I can't see it myself.

There's not much to be done
for an ache
but wait for it to ease.
In the meantime
a layer of skin covers it over,
smooths everything out.

Rain
does
not fall
in order
to make the corn grow
any more than it falls to spoil.

Annie's writing box

holds the memory things:
unused note papers, a set of goose feather
quill pens, her mother-of-pearl-handled
penknife, an unposted letter, a stick
of red sealing wax, her silver thimble, a ribbon
studded with glass beads, a paper folded
over a lock of light-brown hair, a paper folded
over two withered yellow crocuses
her mother cut for her.

Of late

it seems there has been no time;
it has been dragged
along with everything we cannot
think of – night and day
all forms of illumination – deep
into the vortex of her,
our one for the ages. Being still
so young she is in no hurry to let go.
Nor are we
concerned by this. Without time,
events fail to transpire.
We are left
to our own devices.
On the whole we remain
curled into each other
half-hearted
attempting (as we must)
to repair ourselves.

Days, grouped together

May. An exhibition opens,
a king is crowned. A great flood
washes away a small town,
ruining crops.

June. A game of chess.

July. A poisoner caught in the act.
An asteroid, long suspected,
is finally seen. A rush is made
for gold.

Today

as usual I woke
with the thought of her
but managed to let her go from me
for two hours in the morning
and work. She was not
on my mind and then
she was again.

This time it is you have left me behind

yet I expect to see your face,
hear the rattle of your small booted feet on the stairs,
your calling on me please to wait, that you are coming.

With each early blackbird's song, memory revives,
slicing and spilling every dawn's promise as it breaks,
as I expect to see your face – how to bear that I will not?

My first girl, my good girl,
running late, stumbling the length of the hall
calling on me please to wait, that you are coming

and there you are, bonnet awry,
satin ribbons streaming and your bonny, smiling face,
I still expect to see that face – how to bear that I will not? –

Cage-crazed, I seek in corners for a way to unmake
etherised June-May-days, fashion in their place some impossible path
back to you calling on me please to wait, that you are coming.

Monstrous is my heart, without wit or will to stop with yours,
for I no longer wish to be
yet expect to see your face, hear you
calling on me please to wait, that you are coming back to me.

Darwin's first reader

Did she turn your pile of papers
face down on the table? Did she say
she would rather have you
and everyone else in your world
continue to believe, and hang all
your evidence, your findings related
to the beaks and feathers of pigeons,
the behaviour of bees? Did she ask
then what's the point of all this,
what of our three children dead,
what of the Churchman's guarantee
we would see them again?

I can see you before you do it
(and you mean to do it)
standing at her elbow with your theory.
She hasn't noticed you yet,
she's playing the piano with such feeling.
You pause, uncertain now
if you're up to the task.

Battle of the vegetables

For July the weather has been dire;
today the children, bless them,
have been rampaging all morning
along the hallway outside my study door,
waging war. If I understand correctly

Franky leads the carrot army,
little Lenny the potato one,
whilst Lizzy is engaging in a guerrilla action
somewhere between the two,
and all advancing and falling back,
all the time shouting, oh the shouting
and the banging of those wooden swords
which I confess I do regret, as Emma foresaw I would.

Just this instant we have a lull in hostilities,
for I have handed over several sheets
from my manuscript, a slaughtered first draft,
some pens and India ink. Next they will be after
Etty for her watercolours, which is all to the good,
as it will entail them decamping upstairs,
and I shall have peace down here, for a time at least.

The billiard table

Full-sized, with the latest slate bed technology
sourced from Hopkins and Stephens, Covent Garden
for fifty-three pounds eighteen shillings,
which is reasonable considering the quality,
and he covers the cost with funds
from the sale of his father's gold watch
and a few bas-relief Greek figures,
oh and a Wedgewood Barberini vase that,
as he points out to Emma, has only been
gathering dust on the drawing room shelf.

It arrives, broken down into its component parts,
having rolled the twenty miles from London
strapped to the back of a cart. He shouts
to the gardener's boy toiling behind the greenhouse
to help unload, and after an hour
the long limbs are laid out sequentially on the carpet,
like a gigantic mahogany skeleton
some other giant has torn apart.
Two more hours, and the eight-legged framework
stands upright, only slightly unsteady.

Wriggling into a prone position beneath,
he begins sketching a detailed underside view
of the complex screw levelling mechanism
to send to his son George, away at school,
so he too can admire the design and fine craftsmanship.

Once his wool-baize-clad beauty is finally stable,
feet precisely levelled to the lifts and falls
of uneven oak floorboards, he starts in on
his new, full-colour book, also delivered from London,
the one with the detailed diagrams of various cue strokes.
He enjoys spending his free hours practising his moves,
delighting in every carefully judged carom,
the satisfaction of the well rounded click, clunk, plop
of a strike and rebound into a corner pocket.

Nightly after dinner now comes the new ritual,
the lighting of the lamps to shine on coloured balls,
on the small brown heads of his younger sons,
the grey of Parslow the butler,
the sometimes balding ones of visiting scientists,
and so it goes

until the morning he has another idea
and, dragging a heavy sheet from the linen press,
throws it over the baize, carries in
box after box and carefully unwraps
his collection of boiled rabbit bones, dozens
of small femurs and scapula, chopstick-thin ribs,
ovate skulls, arranging each small, creamy fragment
precisely, so they almost touch, in five size-graduated
rows, stretching from one end rail to the other.

Early morning on the Sand-walk

Down House, March 1857

Praise be for fan-tailed pigeons, for flies
who lay their eggs in the navels of animals,
and every parasite that clings to life,

for red-grouse the colour of heather,
black-grouse that of peaty earth,
for the abundance of hair on the breast of the wild turkey,

the inherited peculiarities of the horns on cattle,
for tidal floods of starlings in massed tumblings
across winter skies, for the plumed seed that is wafted.

Praise be for brown beetles diving in streams,
for the wolf pack in snow,
hard pressed for food,

for upland geese with webbed feet
who seldom go near the water, for the beak
and tongue of the woodpecker,

for humble bees sucking at red clover blooms,
for each form, lightly chalked upon a wall,
divided into great branches, oddly perfect.

A short note from brother Erasmus in London

Charles, there is a mysterious box
come for you, marked glass

but with a kind of grid iron lid

as if it had something alive inside.

Observations on their habits

It's true, I didn't like the idea at first. But
the billiard table makes a surprisingly serviceable
home for the master's live earthworm collection
and I've become accustomed
to dusting around them. Only this morning

I witnessed Master Francis
pacing the length of the table whilst
sounding a series of long notes on his bassoon,
the baby joining in with his loud squealing
on Miss Ettie's old tin whistle. Then

Mrs Darwin was prevailed upon to lay down
her needlework and do her part,
a request she met with a short-ish piece on piano
(one of Mr Chopin's *Nocturnes*, she told me later)
performed as loudly as she could manage. For his trick,

Mr Darwin got nose to nose with the creatures
and let loose a barrage of boisterous shouts but,
save for when the force of his expelled breath
puffed against their skin, the worms were, by all
appearances, oblivious to the family's efforts.

A cipher of a man

The evidence that the late Mr Darwin
was the real author of the poems
attributed to Lord Tennyson
does not need the corroboration of any cryptogram;

but if it did, Miss Lesbia Hume, of Earlswood,
has authorised me to say
that she would be prepared to supply
any amount of evidence to that effect.

In the poem 'The Princess', the evidence
derivable from allusions to proper names –
that of the real author
and that of the pretender – is obvious.

The princess asks if the prince has nothing to occupy his time –
'quoit, tennis, ball – no games?'
The prince hears a voice crying to him
'Follow, follow, thou shalt win.'

Here we find half the name of Darwin – the latter half –
and two thirds of the name of Tennyson – the first and second third –
at once associated, contrasted, and harmonised
for those who can read the simplest of cryptograms.

His mind is of the German type:
speculative, laborious and unsound.

The entire subject of his enquiry
is unphilosophical and
impenetrable.

It's for lads who go to popular lectures
given by men with big, ugly pictures,
making nasty smells with bottles and squirts
and calling that anatomy or chemistry.

I don't want to hear
anything more of those
monkey-men.

Twelve voices

But Dearest, how does
he know the monkey
was not once the man?
Surely the downward
road is the easier to
travel? Perhaps
that is the warning
for us?

I gather from scientific men
his view cannot ever claim to be more
than a hypothesis. The whole matter
seems very ingenious and amusing
but I have not time for it;
I would rather read some Italian history.

Refute Darwinism? To what end?
One does not refute fairy tales.

My nephew by marriage came to me,
having read Malthus, then Darwin,
and doubting the goodness of God.
From that time he began to show
symptoms of insanity — which disease,
it is thought, he inherited
from one of his progenitors.
Dressed always in black, he said
he was in mourning for mankind.

It seems to me
one of the threatening clouds
of our day, fascinating
to a certain class of mind.
I fear it will wreck the faith of many.

over five courses

But surely we cannot go
on thinking
the peacock's plumage
has been so richly drawn
solely to please
the admiring eye of man?

What if Darwin be right?
What if the phenomena
you quote
only *simulate*
the preconception
of a definite design,
as flame seems
to incorporate the desire
to ascend,
and water the reverse?

I cannot feel any interest in it.
Of what practical use, to know
my first ancestor may, or may not,
have been an oyster? I am not an oyster.
There is nothing to be gained, for this
world or the next,
by going into this oyster question.

But you must see how he takes
common things, things other men
waste, and out of them makes
the grandest material?

Bee

You've been buzzing and batting your wings against
the inside of my half-open window all morning.

You remind me of a fine pike I observed
at the Regent's Park aquarium,

the one a passing fish-keeper confided
had for months been intent

on dashing himself
just like that, exactly like that, sir,

against his plate glass walls
all in pursuit of the shiny minnows

he could see swimming by yet still somehow
unreachable. Happily perhaps,

nature is not always this way.
Caged weaver birds seem content

busying their beaks and feet
with winding threads of grass

between the wires of their prison cells.
Beavers without a river to dam

will keep themselves occupied
with cutting up logs and dragging them about.

Doubtless the spider whose web
I swung my careless arm through

this morning on the Sandwalk
will, by tomorrow when I pass, have set to

and rebuilt from the ruins,
to the same design, in the same sheltered spot

between privet hedge and gatepost.
Enough with you now, bee.

Look, I have opened the window wider
for you. Take your liberty.

iii

Paper wings

The paper artist is folding cranes,
precision creasing

origami paper squares
printed with geometric shapes

into bright, kimono-robed birds.
The birds nest together

on the coffee table, rustling
to each other: when will she stop?

Five cranes means a sudden
shaft of sunlight,

ten, a day of sunshine
in the middle of this long winter,

a thousand and she will
have her dearest wish.

No, not the impossible one.
That

is beyond
two thousand paper wings.

Rose

Watching them licking their plates at the end of a meal
I wish for more privacy. Mad Henry, as he tired of people,
chopped off their heads. I think he was onto something
but that way anguish lies. A friend once told me
love is like falling from a cliff knowing you have wings.
This is the only time I will repeat that story. I regret not
working harder, but there you have it. Remnants
of peanut butter and baguette. I'm not giving up.

You'd never think to look at him

He's a ditch digger, a share milker, a psychiatrist, he works at the University as a lab technician, he's an electrician, he's a PhD student with a particular interest in the economics of European integration, he has three children of his own, he has no children of his own, he is a step-parent of two teenagers, two toddlers, he is a foster parent who cares for at-risk children who have been removed from their biological parents, he lives alone, he lives with his elderly parents, he lives with his wife and six children, three of whom are hers, he lives with his boyfriend who is much younger than him, who is much older than him, who is more or less the same age, he enjoys tinkering with old motorbikes, he's no good with engines, he once played the role of Joyboy in *West Side Story*, he has a good singing voice although not good enough to go professional, he can't dance, he likes cats but not dogs, he likes dogs but not birds, he particularly hates pigeons, he has a large music collection, mostly jazz and opera, he doesn't like opera, he enjoys going to nightclubs, he prefers a quiet corner in the pub, he grew a beard in his twenties to cover up a scar, he has always been clean shaven, he likes to ski, he likes to read poetry on rainy weekends, he likes to visit art galleries, he can never bring himself to care for modern art, he dislikes museums because the staring eyes of stuffed animals make him feel queasy, on weekends he likes to go horse riding, tramping, to movies that involve car chases and explosions, he prefers European films, especially French comedies, they always have such interesting endings, he's an organ donor, he gives blood, he doesn't give blood because he doesn't like needles, he doesn't give blood because he lived in Wales in the early nineties and the Blood Service won't take his blood because of the very small risk he is a carrier of mad cow disease, he has no visible means of support, he owns the best house in the worst street, he rents the worst house in the best street, he enjoys gardening, he walks to work every day, rain or shine, he takes his car most days, he likes to drive fast, he drinks coffee but never after two in the afternoon, he drinks chamomile tea as coffee gives him headaches, he will not eat mushrooms because they give him a rash, he's been a vegetarian for over seven years, he's eaten meat all his life but has often thought about giving it up, he was brought up Catholic but no longer takes communion, he goes to synagogue twice a week, his wife is Jewish too, he's not married, he has no religious affiliations but is spiritual, he'd like to find more time to just be himself, most of the time he's happy in his life, often he finds he does not like himself, he has lots of friends but no one really knows him well, he has only a few close friends but those he has feel they know him better than they know themselves.

In which his crisis arrives unannounced

Looking out through the lounge room window,
Philip took off his reading glasses to get
a clearer view of the yacht club teenagers
guiding their fleet of P-class dinghies
towards the lakeshore. Many had been gone

for hours. It had been a sunny afternoon
but the pine-scented evening was drawing in,
the last of the daylight etching itself
upon the clouds, those heavy, low-slung
ghosts of a day finally played out.

A single pair of cockeyed swans
occupied themselves with paddling slowly
along the shoreline, ironing the dark
water with their grey-feathered bellies.
Anne bustled in just then to ask if he wanted

to add anything to her Christmas email to the children
but Philip found he could not speak for watching
those young sailors, their arms straining,
their faces in the dusk becoming bright, oval disks
turning from sail to shore and back again.

Of mice and men

I heard a clicking, shifting sound in the long grass today
that made me think again of your recent theory
about your father, long estranged, who died last year,

that he may have murdered a man, back in '78.
More specifically, that he may have killed your
next-door neighbour, the one with the withered arm.

I thought you'd gone a bit mad, but agreed
to think about it and try to recall any little details
that might help you work it out, one way or the other.

I mostly remember your pet mice,
and how mum would make me wash my hands
as soon as I got home from playing at your place.

The neighbour I don't remember much at all,
just a sense of being waved at, that we'd wave back.
I don't think I ever knew his name. Often,

when I'd come over after school, he'd be out
working in his garden and one year, I remember,
his corn plants got so high they nearly covered him

and I can't help feeling, now you've said it,
there was something strange about him dying
like that. The way your mum, looking over the fence

from the clothes line that morning, saw him,
spreadeagled on his back in striped pyjamas,
precisely at the centre of a crop circle of flattened stalks.

This way for the gas

They've been dragging bodies, dead or alive,
off trains again while a ghost
of a man in spotless black
with silver collar-tips stands off to one side,

whip in hand. He's bored at the way everyone naked
looks the same but also indelibly different,
the piles of bodies for burning,
the blue–black buzzing flies, the earth

still turning like before
only with polyester–blend
uniforms and brassier decorations,
some with their hats wider than others, some wearing masks.

Seeing him standing there I can't say for sure
I wouldn't run from my own child
if I saw a big enough gap in the fence
if I thought she would slow me down.

How many hours, how many dead
before I started kicking them aside?
What wouldn't I eat, adrift on a wild sea? I think
if I was drowning I'd pull you down with me.

First time on the disassembly line

Lift the flaps to access underneath
and if you're not sure where things go
check the diagrams,
they're pretty self-explanatory.
Brain in that corner,
a disconnected tree,
liver laid out
like a tulip, I always think,
over here. Kidneys,
twinned bean seeds,
and the pancreas, yes,
that thing that looks like a tongue,
all go on this tray.
Get the idea?

What do we do about the limbic system?

Never mind that now,
just pull everything out.
But careful how you go
or you'll end up with intestines
all over the shop. That's what
the bucket's for. Nerves are tricky,
thin

Like tributaries?

little fuckers, they latch on
to the strangest things. Take it slow,
and when you've got them all out,
coil them up in balls, stack them here.

Once you're done with that lot
open up the chest, spread the ribs,
take out the heart,
leave it in that colander,
it needs to drain completely.
Genitalia go in the safe,
here's the key,
make sure you give it back
to me. Leave the eyes alone,

Can we open a window?

they're slippery sods,
not easy the first time.
I'll do them myself later,
while you watch.

Fully informed

Rotate this verse 90 degrees anti-
clockwise to reveal a graph of reported sexual assaults in the
Wellington District
between 1995
and 2010. Note how levels of
sexual violence fluctuate
significantly
from year to year
which is
interesting.
Note also
the lows in the early noughties; additional
research will be required to pinpoint
the causes of this trend.
Publication of this data on page C3 of the *Dominion Post* ensures readers are fully informed

Bombing the National Gallery of Australia

You'd be surprised how easy it is
to get a bomb into the National Gallery of Australia
in your handbag. Don't take it in a backpack,
they take those off you at the front door.
Having said that, today they let this one guy
slip through undetected. He made it
as far as the Sidney Nolan Gallery
before he was spotted by a guard and sent packing.
But a handbag raises no eyebrows, especially
a bright orange leather one tucked under the arm
of a middle-aged woman.

Standing in front of *The Trial* (1947)
there is something about outlaw Ned's
yellow eyes, sideways-looking at the judge
through the slot in his bucket-shaped helmet,
or maybe it's the goat-faced policeman, gold
buttons all down his uniform, the painted view
of green harbour, grey sky, through the arched window,
that makes you glance at the gallery attendant,
who may have been standing on that same spot all day
staring at the chequered floor tiles
the colour of cream and ripe tamarillos.

Keep it together

At first his mouth was clipped shut, like a purse.
Beginning with a glass of water
they soon moved on to another location.
She held his jacket, stroking the suede collar
while he changed entirely. The inner lining
was some kind of silk. On the TV
farmers were coming out of the front doors
of their farmhouses, tutting over their grass,
which had gone from parched to growing too fast
for their liking. She was thinking her time
might be coming and she didn't mean to spoil it
by looking. But there were five white lilies in a vase
on the table, some postage stamps lying ready for licking,
in one corner an abandoned doll.
Rain fell against the window in big drops,
as if poured through an enormous colander,
but in a moment it was over. It was wondrous
really, she told herself, that night.

Vatican shockwaves

11 February 2013

The pope today announced his retirement,
first pontiff to quit for six hundred years;
can we expect cracks in the firmament?

He spoke in Latin, no one knew what he meant
so they got it translated; now it appears
the pope has announced his retirement.

Evidently the gist was 'It's time I went',
at least that's what the world hears
coming through the cracks in the firmament.

A posse of Cardinals conferred, then sent
a trustworthy altar boy to get in the beers,
for the pope had announced his retirement.

The faithful worry: who will now be their parent?
Send someone sober out to allay their fears
and cover up the cracks in the firmament.

Some things people say cannot be meant.
Today, when it rains, it's not really God's tears.
The pope has announced his retirement.
Look up, see the cracks in the firmament.

Underground

You've thought for months it must be
the fridge muttering away to itself.
Tonight, when the rattle wakes you,
you go into the kitchen and switch it off
at the wall, but the faint sound remains.
Kneeling, you place your ear
to the floor and it amplifies then,
something unrelenting
grinding away below the surface.

Not an animal, you decide.
Tunnelling animals are unheard of in these parts
and besides, the vibration is that of a big machine,
something monstrous the height
of four men placed end to end
with a steel mouthful of rotating teeth,
hoses protruding for the extrusion
of grey sand by-product.

You make yourself a cup of tea
warm your hands on the side of the cup
ignoring the ripples forming
on the hot, liquid surface and try not to think
about tunnels, the way, like garden sheds,
they tend to become crowded with things
far beyond those originally intended,
before their eventual descent into disrepair,
echoing, empty of their intended purpose.

Switching the fridge back on
you return to your cooling bed
pull the covers up over your ears.
But now you've heard it, you can't
unhear. It sounds close.

Easter 2014

Three hundred people have just volunteered
to die in order to save the rest of humanity.
That's not how human nature works
I sniff. We keep watching anyway,
eating our eggs, as they slowly expire on screen.
We can tell when they're definitely dead:
one woman has her eyes open, staring. Later,
on our way downtown, we discuss
how Jesus did the same. I say I don't think
he actually died on the cross. I mean,
I think he thought he was going to die, I think
they thought he was dead when they cut him down,
just like that Italian grandmother they found
in a chiller at the morgue, the one
who'd torn the skin on her fingers to shreds trying
to get out. No one visits bodies in the morgue.
But Jesus, his friends visited his tomb.
They must have heard him calling and got him out alive.
We decide it's easy to imagine it: Jesus being
half carried, half dragged home, covered
by a blanket to hide his identity from the mob.
Jesus, gathering Mary and the children close,
leaving town that same night. Because for sure,
if they'd caught him, they'd have nailed him up again.

Delivery suite

It wasn't quite how you'd foreseen this day unfolding
but he has to park the car. The duty midwife
spots you on a security camera, doubled over,
and comes out to get you.

She says *you on your own then?* looking beyond.
No, he's just – parking the car you say between the waves
and as she hauls you upright he trots over,
puffing, and together they support you inside
to a delivery suite, where you sink to all fours on the floor.

You're not going to stay down there are you?
she says. *Only I've got a bad knee.* Enlisting his help,
she gets you back on your feet and you find
you really need to pee so go into the en suite where
you find blood from the woman before you smeared all over the seat and the
bowl and begin to understand how, despite his best intentions,
you're on your own.

★

Finally you ask if you can have some drugs:
a shot of pethidine.

Or anything.

But *oh no dear, we're well past the time
for that kind of thing*

★

You do the business, even though for a while there
you hadn't wanted to be involved, even said quite loudly that
you wanted to go home.

★

But that's over now and your baby's here,
so that's okay, except they're still waiting for the placenta;
the surgeon might have to take you off somewhere in a minute,

which wasn't in the plan for today.

★

If your baby's not feeding it's crying, and has been for hours now.
They offered to take her away in the night
but you didn't want that either –
what if they lost her?

You lie awake, trying to curl yourself around her.

★

At first light you're at the window,
your arms full of baby, watching each car turn into
the front gates, watching for the red one
that's going to take you both away from all this

and, although it's mid-morning before he finally rolls in
and parks, making a meal of detaching the baby seat
from the back seat of the car,
still you whisper in her ear,
That man there, that's your dad,
and hold her up to see.

Acknowledgements

My thanks to the editors of *Sport, Landfall, Turbine, Best New Zealand Poems 2014, Swamp, Hue & Cry, Sweet Mammalian, Penduline Press, The 4th Floor Literary Journal* and *JAAM*, where versions of some of these poems have been published.

A large proportion of this book was written during my 2013 MA year at the International Institute of Modern Letters, Victoria University of Wellington. I am grateful to *The Dominion Post* for their award of an MA by Thesis Scholarship to assist with funding my postgraduate studies. Thank you also to Chris Price and my talented MA classmates for their generous support and encouragement, and to the staff and students of Clyde Quay School Te Kura o Matarangi for being inspirational.

I am particularly grateful to Cambridge University Press and Massey University Library for supplying me with material related to Charles Darwin which proved invaluable in crafting the Darwin sequence of poems.

Thank you James Brown for friendship, insightful comments on early versions of many of these poems, and assorted musical recommendations. Many thanks to Ashleigh Young, Fergus Barrowman and Kirsten McDougall at Victoria University Press for your good humour, enthusiasm and commitment.

Thank you to Viv Baartman, Gavin Baartman and Catherine Foley for being the best friends I could ever wish for, to my family for their love and support (with a special award to my brother for best use of computer programming skills in the pursuit of poetry), and to my husband Greg for all this and more.